HUMBLED

HUMBLED

ELIJAH JOHNSON

Tampa, Florida

The views and opinions expressed in this book are solely those of the author and do not reflect the views or opinions of Gatekeeper Press. Gatekeeper Press is not to be held responsible for and expressly disclaims responsibility of the content herein.

Humbled

Published by Gatekeeper Press
7853 Gunn Hwy, Suite 209
Tampa, FL 33626
www.GatekeeperPress.com

Copyright © 2023 by Elijah Johnson
All rights reserved. Neither this book, nor any parts within it may be sold or reproduced in any form or by any electronic or mechanical means, including information storage and retrieval systems, without permission in writing from the author. The only exception is by a reviewer, who may quote short excerpts in a review.

Library of Congress Control Number: 2022952340

ISBN (paperback): 9781662928147
eISBN: 9781662936333

For CJ

Table of Contents

Apologies	1
You Left	2
Remember	3
Diamond Ring	4
Muse	5
Smell The Rose	6
B.S.	7
On Fire	8
Look In The Mirror	9
Summer	10
Poet	11
Alone	12
Depression	13
Read	15
Write My Mind	16
Words Of Advice	17
We Wear The Scars	18
I've Prayed For Death	19
Hopeless Romantic	20
Paper Cuts For Bleeding Hearts	21
My Wife	22

Blue Eyes	23
September	24
Autumn's Leaves	25
You	26
Love, Lost & Found	27
Autumn	28
Your Turn To Bat	29
Apple Picking Season	30
October	31
Anthem	32
Fair Is Foul	33
Fool's Follow	34
Joyful Hearts	36
Journey	37
New Year	38
Grafton Square Hardware	39
About The Author	41

Apologies

I was wrong and you were right
I didn't know this would ignite
Unsympathetic to your plight
Being strong with all my might
I was surprised at twilight
That you would exit stage right
Behaving so cold, giving me frostbite
Why all these trials you want to indict?
Putting our life in the spotlight
All of the feuding seems so contrite
Taking a break to gain respite
I'm listening now gaining insight
Still in love with you through all this despite
Even if we are just polite
My words were cold I see in hindsight
Always wanting to be your white knight
And our future looked so bright
I stare into the moonlight hoping to reunite,
Until then all I can do is write
Dreaming of the day I can hold you tight.

You Left

You left with the water still running
You never even came back to check
Must be something wrong with the plumbing
I was left with a horrible wreck
I can't seem to handle these issues
I'm not sure I know what to do
Just ran out of all my tissues
All I can think about now is you
I'll do my best here to fix it
And put things back into place
I know we still make a perfect fit
I still miss your beautiful face
My tear drops keep falling like rain
As my heart gets washed down the drain.

Remember

Remember when I said "I love you"
Think of me in a good light
When it was only just us two
Kiss me and let's say "goodnight"

I know we're both tired and upset
And wanting to go separate ways
You are the best person that I've met
And I hope we will have better days

These trials that we have to go through
Are drifting us further apart
Remember when we said our "I Do's"
I love you with all of my heart.

Diamond Ring

Does a diamond have value
After it's lost it's luster?
When you bought it with
Every last cent you could muster

Every piece of your heart
Gets infused in the stone
Your life's investment
Gets put out on loan

If marriage gets tough
And you fall out of favor
Will the diamond still
Be something you savor?

If it should find a home
With a couple starting new
Does a diamond have value
When it means nothing to you?

Muse

In the darkness I find my Muse
You're the one I've always tried to amuse
But you left my heart with a deep bruise
And now I'm the one left singing the blues
If only I was given some sort of clues
Am I just here for you to abuse?
Haven't I already paid all of my dues?
Thinking your love I would never lose
All of this tension I hope to diffuse
Don't think my words are only a ruse
It's you that I need, it's you that I choose.

Smell The Rose

Did you stop and smell the Rose
That was on the tip of your nose?

That you cut off to spite your face
To save yourself from disgrace

You left me all alone
Waiting here by the phone

Needing your time and space
Am I that easy to replace?

Do you ever think of me and frown?
I'm the Rose you let fall to the ground.

B.S.

I wasn't born with a rose colored glass
I was given a blue one instead
Just because I let your b.s. fly past
Doesn't mean I forgot what you said
Every time you damaged my soul
I bottled the hurt up inside
After all this kind of abuse
I find it hard to let slide.

On Fire

For all the love I gave
You turned
You threw a match
And watched me burn
You did not go
To look and see
Or even try
To rescue me
For the fire you
Gave me blame
Perhaps I'll never
Be the same
You did not care
For me one bit
That's why you left
And called it quit
Although my wounds
Took time to heal
Now my heart
Is tempered steel.

Look In The Mirror

Just stop with the daggers
I've already staggered
You say it's my fault
Caught in your verbal assault
I see through your game
It's me who you'll blame
With your need to be right
There is always a fight
You are quick to unload
When I take the high road
If you want to see clearer
Take a good look in the mirror.

Summer

I smell citronella
In the night
And fireflies the
Only light
Crickets chirp
A lovely song
Summer vacation
Seems so long
Fireworks across
The sky
Remembering a time
Once by
Warm enough for
Iced tea
And fried clams
By the sea
Children run and
Splash and play
Wishing Summer was
Everyday.

Poet

The world is full of poets
With their own story to tell
Routinely putting on faces
Their lives they try to sell
They easily draw inspiration
From a deep emotional well
You always can tell a great poet
Who's gone through their own hell.

Alone

Alone with my thoughts
Alone in the world
Into a lonely part
Of my mind I curl
In a dark corner
Of a deep place
Why does the darkness
Rent so much space?
Holding back tears
Struggling to breathe
This is what it must
Feel like to grieve
Stuck in a prison
Of my own guilt
Losing every positive
Memory I've built
Wanting to SCREAM!
But, my inner voices
Only groan
This is how it feels
Being all alone.

Depression

In smokey fog
And misty fens
To see the world
Through a dark lens

Ominous clouds above
Down pouring rain
Wanting joy and
Receiving pain

Tangled weeds
Strangle life
Working hard
For only strife

Glass half empty
All the time
Craving more
Seems a crime

In my room
On darkened bed
Trying to escape
My head

Heaven sent or
Devil's seed
It only comes
Around to feed

The tallest bridge
My only action
I won't give it
The satisfaction.

Read

The world is
In sorest need
Of people who
Love to read
Not just old
Men in tweed
But the new
Growing breed
Planting a deep
Rooted seed
Some sound advice
To take heed
Those most likely
To succeed
Will become the
Liberated freed.

Write My Mind

Speak your mind
I'll write mine instead
Just to ensure the message
Gets widespread
Conformity has always
Been something I dread
Being my own person
Not easily misled
I'd rather be crazy
Than to be over-med
I'll write down my feelings
So they aren't left unsaid.

Words Of Advice

Here are some words of advice
That I was once taught

Time is moving forward
If you like it or not

Try to keep pace
Shit or get off the pot

Better make it count
You only get one shot

What you never want to hear
Is should've, could've, ought.

We Wear The Scars

We are the tired and weary
Those who see the world clearly
Sometimes getting by just barely
In breaking our backs daily

What for all this hard toil?
To be laid six feet in soil
In servitude or loyal
The world is greased in oil

Does the sky determine our fate?
An old man with keys to a gate
Pay now before it's too late
Or suffer at an eternal rate

It's not from karma of stars
Or little green men from Mars
Maybe the fault is just ours
Hurting others we wear the scars.

I've Prayed For Death

I've prayed for death
That never came
Watched my life
Go down the drain
When I needed help
No one was sane
Hoped for sun
And found only rain
So I found the
Heart to train
Myself to live
Alongside the pain.

Hopeless Romantic

I am a hopeless romantic
Hopeless to ever find romance
Staring out the window daydreaming
Waiting for my turn to dance
I hope someday I'll find you
Maybe love at first glance
I'll just have to keep waiting
For someone to give me a chance.

Paper Cuts For Bleeding Hearts

Paper cuts for bleeding hearts
Turning into saddened thoughts
Letter marked with tear drop spots
Inspiration shoots it's poison dart
Showing where creativity starts
Heartbreak Muse's greatest art.

My Wife

My wife is a jewel of the Nile
Who yells only once in a while
I give her a smile
And plead my denial
She keeps all her complaints on file.

Blue Eyes

Into her blue eyes
I can hear the waves crashing
And smell the ocean.

September

How crisp and clean the Autumn air
Farmers market on the square
Wheat fields sway in gentle breeze
Apples fall from boughs with ease
Picked an aster for September's queen
The fairest maiden on Terra's green.

Autumn's Leaves

Autumn's leaves
Are very bold
As jealous Winter's
Eyes behold
Nature's amber and
Brilliant gold
Boasts her beauty
As seasons unfold.

You

You are a phoenix
Burning bright
Turning darkness
Into light
A storm out on
An open sea
A peaceful calm
Tranquility
If there's one thing
I hope you'll see
You are the definition
Of poetry.

Love, Lost & Found

When you become stubborn and
Stand your ground

What you once thought was
Airtight, solid and sound

Left on the last flight
Right out of town

You grieve a tough loss
And come back rebound

Much better equipped
For this time around

What might seem trivial
Could be quite profound

That nothing is better
Than love, lost and found.

Autumn

Leaves gently falling
Covering the ground yellow
Like a warm blanket.

Your Turn To Bat

Step right up
To the plate
It's your turn to bat

Don't just sit there
On the bench
Fidgeting your hat

We only need
One more run
To be in the lead

If you don't
Take the bat
You'll never succeed

Sometimes you will
Step out of your
Comfort zone of zen

Even the best
Strike out seven
Out of ten.

Apple Picking Season

Can you smell the apples
On the ground?

McIntosh I think
They are

Birds are singing
A sweet sound

Heaven doesn't seem
So far

Sit down with me
By the fire

There is room
Enough for two

I'll share my cup
Of apple cider

And spend the
Afternoon with you.

October

Falling leaves are bittersweet
Dew drop grass under feet
Children in costumes
Going "Trick or Treat"
Pumpkin pie, hot apple cider
Not much in the world is finer
Football games under stadium lights
Spooky movie popcorn nights
Golden light makes birds sing
Pumpkin flavored everything!

Anthem

I've lived and
I've loved,
got pushed and
shoved
knocked down
and still
rose above.

Fair Is Foul

Often youth is foul faced
Of which and not
Is up to taste
Their gold standard
For all is based
Fleeting thought
Is soon erased
And laurel crowned
Victory chased
Yet wisdom moves at
Slower pace
What once was fair is
Now disgraced.

Fool's Follow

I give free advice
For fool's to follow
You can come see me
Or a bar stool to wallow
I might seem harsh
A tough pill to swallow
The world isn't a good place
To be a marshmallow
All the roads lead
Six feet below
I charge no fee
It just fuels my ego
Come on and sit down
My worrisome fellow
Is it money or women?
That might seem the trouble
"Both!" Yes indeed
"Which way should I go?"
Why do you ask me?
How the hell should I know?
I have lost both
And cry in my pillow

It's through the hard times
That we learn to grow
You'll notice the broken,
The stoic and shallow
The blank expressionless
Ice in their marrow
Burned by advice of the
Sage and the guru
Answers to questions
You already knew
I give free advice
For fool's to follow.

Joyful Hearts

Cups of cocoa
Falling flakes
Children playing
On ice skates
Snowmen made
Clean and white
Presents will
Arrive tonight
Joyful hearts
And glad tidings
On a sleigh
Santa's riding.

Journey

On the   journey
to find   myself
I looked within
and found
You
!

New Year

There are only a few things
I actually fear
Like the passing of each
And every new year
It's time to put my
Life into gear
And only look forward
Never the rear
Taking hold of the
Wheel trying to steer
Life sometimes gets bumpy
So try not to veer
I know of one thing that's
Become crystal clear
I'll keep close to my heart
All that I hold dear.

Grafton Square Hardware

When inspiration sparked
Gram's creative mind
Off to the store for what
She could find
Not much for me but
A gum ball machine
And spending time
In Gram's company.

Corner of Hamilton
And down the stairs
All the essentials
For home repairs
Paint and tape or a
Brand new hammer
What's in the mind
Of this feverish planner?

Painting the lamps
And the shades
Change your world
Just for today

And when she found
Her moment of zen
Tomorrow we might
Do it again.

About The Author

I am a Marine Corps veteran
and graduate of Becker College.
I am a native of Worcester,
Massachusetts and have one son.

www.ingramcontent.com/pod-product-compliance
Lightning Source LLC
LaVergne TN
LVHW011900060526
838200LV00054B/4443